Pebble® Plus

## Dance, Dance, Dance

# Hip-Hop Dancing

by Kathryn Clay

Consulting editor: Gail Saunders-Smith, PhD

Content consultant: Heidi L. Schimpf,
Director of Programs and Services
Joy of Motion Dance Center
Washington, D.C.

CAPSTONE PRESS
a capstone imprint

Pebble Plus is published by Capstone Press,
151 Good Counsel Drive, P.O. Box 669, Mankato, Minnesota 56002.
www.capstonepress.com

092009
005618CGS10

 Books published by Capstone Press are manufactured with paper
containing at least 10 percent post-consumer waste.

*Library of Congress Cataloging-in-Publication Data*
Clay, Kathryn.
　Hip-hop dancing / by Kathryn Clay.
　　p. cm. — (Pebble plus. Dance, dance, dance)
　Includes bibliographical references and index.
　Summary: "Simple text and photographs present hip-hop dancing, including simple steps" — Provided
by publisher.
　　ISBN 978-1-4296-4003-9 (library binding)
　　1. Hip-hop dance. I. Title.
GV1796.H57C57 2010
792.8 — dc22
　　　　　　　　　　　　　　　　　　　　　　2009023385

**Editorial Credits**
Jennifer Besel, editor; Veronica Bianchini, designer; Marcie Spence, media researcher;
　Eric Manske, production specialist

**Photo Credits**
All photos by Capstone Studio/Karon Dubke

**The Capstone Press Photo Studio thanks Dance Express in
Mankato, Minnesota, and The Dance Connection in Rosemount,
Minnesota, for their help with photo shoots for this book.**

## Note to Parents and Teachers

The Dance, Dance, Dance series supports national physical education standards and the
national standards for learning and teaching dance in the arts. This book describes and
illustrates hip-hop dancing. The images support early readers in understanding the text. The
repetition of words and phrases helps early readers learn new words. This book also introduces
early readers to subject-specific vocabulary words, which are defined in the Glossary section.
Early readers may need assistance to read some words and to use the Table of Contents,
Glossary, Read More, Internet Sites, and Index sections of the book.

# Table of Contents

# All about Hip-Hop

Drop to the floor,

and pop back up.

Hip-hop dance is full of energy.

Hip-hop dancers move
to hip-hop music.
Hip-hop music mixes rap
and fast beats.

# What to Wear

Hip-hop dancers wear T-shirts, baggy pants, and shorts. Loose clothing makes it easy to move.

Hip-hop dancers

wear sneakers.

Sneakers keep dancers

from slipping

on the floor.

# Sweet Steps

Take a step to the right

with your right foot.

Slide your left toes on the floor

to meet your right foot.

This move is called a toe drag.

Pull your elbows up

to your sides and freeze.

This move is called locking.

Point one foot in front of you.

Rock your body

back and forth.

This move is called top rocking.

Drop down

like you're doing a push-up.

Then kick your legs wide.

This move is called

the drop and kick out.

## Ready to Dance

Lock, rock, and show off

your moves.

You're hip-hop dancing!

# Glossary

**baggy** — hanging loosely

**beat** — the rhythm of a piece of music

**drag** — to pull something along the ground

**freeze** — to hold still

**rap** — a type of song in which the words are spoken to the music

# Read More

**Clay, Kathryn.** *Jazz Dancing.* Dance, Dance, Dance. Mankato, Minn.: Capstone Press, 2010.

**Karapetkova, Holly.** *Dance.* Sports for Sprouts. Vero Beach, Fla.: Rourke, 2010.

# Internet Sites

FactHound offers a safe, fun way to find Internet sites related to this book. All of the sites on FactHound have been researched by our staff.

Here's all you do:

Visit *www.facthound.com*

FactHound will fetch the best sites for you!

# Index

Word Count: 149
Grade: 1
Early-Intervention Level: 14